this book belong to

MILWAUKEE
6
#6
BLEDSOE

WESLEY MATTHEWS
BUCKS
9

KHRIS MIDDLETON 22

LAKERS
24

GIANNIS
34

DON
45

PAT CONNAUGHTON

BRYANT
24

32

THANASIS ANTETOKOUNMPO

LeBron James

BULLS
23

CAM REYNOLDS

CITY
13

STERLING BROWN
BUCKS
23

RAPTORS
2

ROBIN LOPEZ
11
MILWAUKEE
42

BROOK LOPEZ

THE
BIG
RAGU
BUCKS
0
#0

ERSAN ILYASOVA

THUNDER

WARRIORS
11

fitbit
WOLVES
23

KYLE KORVER

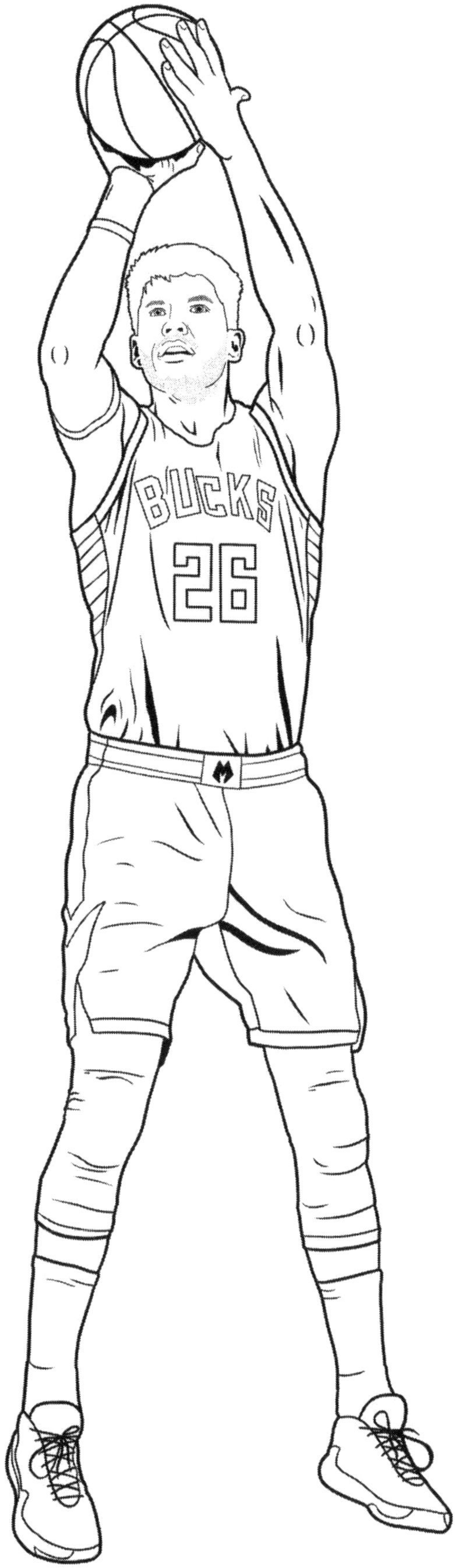

GOLDE
23
WARRIORS

BOSTON
11

BULLS
45

Made in United States
Troutdale, OR
12/11/2024

26309139R00035